UNLOCK THE KEYS TO SELF-MOTIVATION

ACHIEVING YOUR DREAMS

DR. JAGADEESH PILLAI

Copyright © Dr. Jagadeesh Pillai
All Rights Reserved.

This book has been self-published with all reasonable efforts taken to make the material error-free by the author. No part of this book shall be used, reproduced in any manner whatsoever without written permission from the author, except in the case of brief quotations embodied in critical articles and reviews.

The Author of this book is solely responsible and liable for its content including but not limited to the views, representations, descriptions, statements, information, opinions and references ["Content"]. The Content of this book shall not constitute or be construed or deemed to reflect the opinion or expression of the Publisher or Editor. Neither the Publisher nor Editor endorse or approve the Content of this book or guarantee the reliability, accuracy or completeness of the Content published herein and do not make any representations or warranties of any kind, express or implied, including but not limited to the implied warranties of merchantability, fitness for a particular purpose. The Publisher and Editor shall not be liable whatsoever for any errors, omissions, whether such errors or omissions result from negligence, accident, or any other cause or claims for loss or damages of any kind, including without limitation, indirect or consequential loss or damage arising out of use, inability to use, or about the reliability, accuracy or sufficiency of the information contained in this book.

Made with ♥ on the Notion Press Platform
www.notionpress.com

|| Dedicated to all wisdom seekers around the world ||

ᕳᕳᕳ

Contents

Contents

Prayer

**"Om Bhadram Karnebhih Shrunuyaama
DevaahBhadram Pashyemaakshabhiryajatraah
SthirairangaistushtuvaamsastanoobhihVyashema
Devahitam YadaayuhSwasti Na Indro
VridhashravaahSwasti Nah Pooshaa
VishwavedaahSwasti Nastaarkshyo ArishtanemihSwasti
No Brihaspatir DadhaatuOm Shantih, Shantih, Shantih"**

The literal meaning of this mantra is: OM. O Gods! Let us
hear auspicious words from our ears. O reverent Gods! Let
us behold propitious visions from our eyes, let our organs
and body be stable, healthy, and strong. Let us do that
which is pleasing to the gods in the life span allotted to us.
May Indra, inscribed in the scriptures, bring us fortune!
May Pushan, the knower of the world, grant us prosperity!
May Trakshya, who vanquishes enemies, bestow us with
blessings! May Brihaspati bring us success!
OM Peace, Peace, Peace.

ॐॐॐ

About The Author

Dr. Jagadeesh Pillai is a renowned Guinness World Record holder, writer, and researcher hailing from Varanasi, also known as the abode of Lord Shiva. With a Ph.D. in Vedic Science and a range of creative ideas and achievements, he is a true polymath. He is the author of more than 100 books including Research Publications. Although his roots can be traced back to Kerala, the people of Varanasi hold him in high regard and affectionately consider him one of their own.

In 1998, Dr. Pillai was offered a job at Banaras Hindu University, but he left the position after only two months to pursue greater goals in life. He believed that in order to study Indian scriptures and engage in other creative endeavours, he needed to retire from the daily grind of working solely for money at a young age.

He started an export business from scratch, using the knowledge he had gained from a previous job in the industry. His intelligence and unique approach to business led to great success in a short period of time, earning him more in just a decade and a half than he would have in a lifetime working in a government job. Upon the passing of Dr. APJ Abdul Kalam, Dr. Pillai decided to leave the business and dedicate himself to reading, studying, researching, and experimenting.

During his tenure in the export business, Dr. Pillai traveled to over 16 countries, gaining valuable insight and experiencing the world and life in detail.

Dr. Pillai has achieved four Guinness World Records in the following subjects:

"Script to Screen" - In this record, Dr. Pillai produced and directed an animation film within the shortest time possible, breaking the previous record set by Canadians. He has also received numerous national and international awards and recognitions for this achievement.

Longest Line of Postcards - For this record, Dr. Pillai created a line of 16,300 postcards on the occasion of the 163rd anniversary of Indian Postal Day. The event also included a questionnaire about the Indian flag.

Largest Poster Awareness Campaign - Dr. Pillai designed an awareness campaign on the subject of "Beti Bachao - Beti Padhao" (Save the Girl Child - Educate the Girl Child) to achieve this record.

Largest Envelope - In tribute to the Indian Prime Minister's "Make in India" initiative, Dr. Pillai created a 4000 square meter envelope using waste paper to achieve this record.

Attempted - **70000 Candles on a 210 kg Cake** - To celebrate the 70th Indian Independence Day, Dr. Pillai attempted to light 70,000 candles on a 210 kg cake, which was recorded in World Records India.

Attempted - **Documentary on Dhamek Stupa of Sarnath in 17 Languages** - Dr. Pillai attempted to create a documentary on the Dhamek Stupa of Sarnath, dubbing it in 17 different languages. The result of this attempt is currently awaiting confirmation from the Guinness World Records.

Dr. Pillai is skilled in teaching the Bhagavad Gita, a Hindu scripture, and is popular among young people. He has helped many young people improve their lives through his motivational teachings.

In addition to teaching, he has composed and sung numerous Sanskrit Bhajans and patriotic songs.

He has also written and directed several short films and documentaries for awareness campaigns, and has volunteered with the police in both UP and Kerala to spread awareness about various issues through videos and photography.

Incredibly, he has produced and directed over 100 documentaries about the city of Varanasi, all on his own.

He has also helped and guided more than 25 boys and girls to achieve world records through creative and innovative methods. He is a multifaceted person who uses his intellect and the blessings given to him by God to excel in various areas. He is both a teacher and a student, always learning and teaching, and is able to master any subject he comes across.

He is a selfless social activist and motivational speaker who has overcome struggles and failures to become a successful and enthusiastic individual with a rich life experience.

In addition to his work with the Bhagavad Gita, he is also an efficient Tarot card reader, Astro-Vastu consultant, and a talented singer and composer. He has sung the entire Ram Charita Manas and Bhagavad Gita in his own compositions, and has sung the phrase "Lokah Samastha Sukhino Bhavantu" in 50 different languages. He is currently working on a detailed and scientific study of Vedas, Upanishads, Puranas, and the Bhagavad Gita. He has also composed and sung the Hanuman Chalisa and Gayatri Mantra in 108 and 1008 different compositions, respectively.

Awards - Four Times Guinness World Records, Winner of Mahatma Gandhi Vishwa Shanti Puraskar, Mahatma Gandhi Global Peace Ambassador, Kashi Ratna Award, Dr. APJ Abdul Kalam Motivational Person of the Year 2017, Mother Teresa Award, Indira Gandhi Priyadarshini Award, Bharat Vikas Ratna Award, Udyog Ratna Award, Vigyan Prasar Award, Poorvanchal Ratn Samman.

ॐॐॐ

Preface

Welcome to the "Secrets of Mastering the Art of Self-Motivation: A Guide to Achieving Your Goals". Self-motivation is a critical ingredient for success in all areas of life. It is the driving force that helps you overcome obstacles, pursue your passions, and reach your full potential. However, despite its importance, self-motivation can be difficult to achieve and maintain, especially in the face of life's many challenges and distractions.

This book is designed to help you unlock the secrets of self-motivation and achieve your goals, no matter what they may be. It provides a comprehensive overview of the key concepts, strategies, and techniques that can help you cultivate and sustain self-motivation. From setting and sticking to goals, to overcoming fears and anxiety, to developing self-discipline and positive habits, this book covers it all.

Additionally, the book explores a range of powerful tools and techniques, including visualization, positive self-talk, self-care, and meditation, that can help you tap into your inner strength and reach new heights of self-motivation and personal fulfillment. Whether you are a student, a professional, or simply someone looking to achieve more in life, this book will provide you with the tools, knowledge, and inspiration you need to succeed.

So, if you are ready to take control of your life, achieve your goals, and unleash your full potential, this book is for you. So, buckle up, and let's begin the journey towards mastering the art of self-motivation.

❤❤❤

ONE

Understanding the Basics of Self-Motivation

Self-motivation is the key to unlocking your full potential and achieving your goals. To master the art of self-motivation, it's important to understand the basics. In this chapter, you will learn what self-motivation is, why it's important, and how to cultivate it within yourself.

What is Self-Motivation?

Self-motivation refers to the drive that comes from within to initiate and maintain action towards a goal. It's a combination of our thoughts, emotions, and behaviors that propels us forward and keeps us focused on what we want to achieve. Unlike external motivation, which comes from external sources such as rewards or punishments, self-motivation is an internal process that stems from our own values, beliefs, and aspirations.

Why is Self-Motivation Important?

Self-motivation is crucial because it provides the energy and drive we need to overcome obstacles and reach our goals. Without self-motivation, it's easy to become discouraged and give up when faced with challenges. Self-motivation also helps us stay focused and committed to our goals, even when the going gets tough. It enables us to take control of our own lives and achieve our aspirations, rather than being at the mercy of external circumstances.

How to Cultivate Self-Motivation

Clarify your goals: Start by defining what you want to achieve and why it's important to you. Write down your goals and keep them in a visible place to keep you motivated.

Develop a growth mindset: Believe in your own ability to grow and improve. Instead of giving up when faced with obstacles, see challenges as opportunities to learn and grow.

Surround yourself with positive influences: Surround yourself with people who support and encourage you. Seek out mentors and role models who inspire you to reach your goals.

Focus on progress, not perfection: Celebrate small wins along the way and focus on progress, rather than perfection.

Keep a positive attitude: Focus on the good in each

situation and maintain a positive outlook, even when things are tough.

In conclusion, self-motivation is the foundation of success and the key to achieving your goals. By understanding the basics and cultivating self-motivation within yourself, you will be well on your way to mastering the art of self-motivation and reaching your full potential.

ᕦᕦᕦ

"The greatest glory in living lies not in never falling, but in rising every time we fall."

- Nelson Mandela

❥❥❥

TWO

WHY SELF-MOTIVATION MATTERS

Self-motivation is a critical component for personal and professional success. It is the drive that comes from within to initiate and maintain action towards a goal. Unlike external motivation, which comes from outside sources such as rewards or punishments, self-motivation stems from one's own values, beliefs, and aspirations. Understanding why self-motivation matters is crucial for anyone looking to achieve their full potential and lead a fulfilling life.

Empowers Personal Growth and Development

Self-motivation empowers personal growth and development by providing the energy and drive needed to overcome obstacles and reach goals. When individuals are self-motivated, they take control of their own lives and are not dependent on external circumstances. This sense of agency leads to increased self-esteem and confidence, which in turn drives further growth and development.

Increases Resilience and Perseverance

Self-motivation also increases resilience and perseverance. When individuals are self-motivated, they are more likely to see challenges as opportunities for growth and learning, rather than giving up when faced with obstacles. This growth mindset allows individuals to maintain focus and commitment, even when the going gets tough, and to persevere towards their goals.

Leads to Greater Satisfaction and Happiness

Self-motivation also leads to greater satisfaction and happiness. When individuals are self-motivated, they are more likely to pursue their passions and interests, rather than being at the mercy of external factors. This sense of purpose and fulfillment leads to increased happiness and life satisfaction.

Improves Performance and Productivity

Finally, self-motivation also improves performance and productivity. When individuals are self-motivated, they are more focused and committed to their goals, leading to increased productivity and better outcomes. In the workplace, self-motivated employees are often more engaged and motivated, leading to improved performance and productivity.

In conclusion, self-motivation matters because it provides the drive and determination necessary to overcome obstacles and reach goals. It empowers personal growth and development, increases resilience and perseverance, leads to greater satisfaction and happiness, and improves performance and productivity. Understanding and cultivating self-motivation within oneself is crucial for anyone looking to achieve their full potential and lead a fulfilling life.

"Success is not final, failure is not fatal: it is the courage to continue that counts."

- Winston Churchill

♡♡♡

THREE

How to Set and Stick to Goals

Goals are essential for personal and professional development and provide a roadmap for success. However, setting goals is only half the battle, sticking to them is where the true challenge lies. Fortunately, there are several strategies that can help individuals set and stick to their goals.

Start with a Clear Vision

The first step in setting and sticking to goals is to have a clear vision of what you want to achieve. This means taking the time to reflect on your aspirations, values, and interests, and identifying what is most important to you. Once you have a clear vision, you can then set SMART goals - Specific, Measurable, Attainable, Relevant, and Time-Bound.

Create a Plan of Action

Once you have set your goals, it is important to create a

plan of action to achieve them. This plan should include a timeline, actionable steps, and specific deadlines. Breaking the goal down into smaller, manageable steps makes it easier to focus on what needs to be done and to track progress.

Monitor Progress Regularly

Regularly monitoring progress is critical to staying on track and making adjustments when needed. Consider setting up regular check-ins, either with yourself or with someone else who can provide accountability and support.

Seek Support and Stay Accountable

Seeking support from friends, family, or a mentor can provide accountability and motivation to stay on track. Surrounding yourself with people who believe in your goals and are invested in your success can make a huge difference.

Embrace a Growth Mindset

Finally, it is important to embrace a growth mindset, where challenges are seen as opportunities for learning and improvement. Keeping a positive mindset and focusing on progress, rather than perfection, can help individuals persist in the face of obstacles and achieve their goals.

In conclusion, setting and sticking to goals requires a clear vision, a plan of action, regular monitoring of progress, seeking support and staying accountable, and embracing a growth mindset. By implementing these strategies, individuals can increase their chances of achieving their goals and lead a fulfilling life.

❦❦❦

"Motivation is the fuel, necessary to keep the human engine running."

- Zig Ziglar

❥❥❥

FOUR

CREATING AN ENVIRONMENT FOR SUCCESS

Creating an environment that supports personal and professional growth is crucial to achieving success. This environment should be designed to foster motivation, productivity, and a positive mindset. Here are several strategies for creating an environment that promotes success:

Surround Yourself with Positive People

Surrounding yourself with positive, supportive people who believe in your goals and values can have a powerful impact on your success. These individuals can offer encouragement, advice, and accountability, and can help you stay motivated when the going gets tough.

Organize Your Workspace

A cluttered, disorganized workspace can be a major source of stress and distraction. On the other hand, a well-organized, clean workspace can increase focus, productivity, and motivation. Take the time to declutter your workspace, organize your supplies and materials, and create a space that is conducive to working and learning.

Limit Distractions

Distractions, such as notifications from your phone or social media, can be a major hindrance to productivity and motivation. Limiting distractions, such as turning off notifications or working in a designated quiet space, can help you stay focused and motivated.

Establish a Routine

Establishing a routine can provide structure and stability, and can help you prioritize your goals and focus on what is most important. Consider creating a daily, weekly, or monthly routine that includes time for work, self-care, and leisure activities.

Celebrate Your Wins

Finally, it is important to celebrate your wins, no matter how small they may be. Celebrating your achievements, big or small, helps to maintain motivation, provides a sense of accomplishment, and keeps you focused on your goals.

In conclusion, creating an environment that supports personal and professional growth is essential for success.

By surrounding yourself with positive people, organizing your workspace, limiting distractions, establishing a routine, and celebrating your wins, you can create an environment that fosters motivation, productivity, and a positive mindset.

❦❦❦

"The only limit to our realization of tomorrow will be our doubts of today."

- Franklin D. Roosevelt

ᐳᐳᐳ

FIVE

OVERCOMING FEARS AND ANXIETY

Fear and anxiety can be major obstacles to success and can prevent individuals from reaching their full potential. Fortunately, there are several strategies that can help individuals overcome their fears and anxieties and achieve their goals.

Identify the Root Causes of Your Fears

The first step in overcoming fear and anxiety is to identify the root causes. This may require some self-reflection and introspection, but it is important to understand what is causing the fear or anxiety in order to address it effectively.

Challenge Negative Thoughts and Beliefs

Fear and anxiety are often rooted in negative thoughts and

beliefs. By challenging these thoughts and beliefs, individuals can start to reframe their experiences in a more positive light. This may involve questioning the evidence for the negative thought, looking for alternative perspectives, or seeking support from others.

Practice Mindfulness and Self-Care

Mindfulness and self-care can be powerful tools for managing fear and anxiety. Practicing mindfulness, such as deep breathing, meditation, or yoga, can help to calm the mind and reduce stress. In addition, taking care of physical and emotional needs, such as getting enough sleep, eating well, and engaging in activities that bring joy, can also help to reduce fear and anxiety.

Seek Professional Help

In some cases, seeking professional help may be necessary to overcome fear and anxiety. A therapist or counselor can provide support, guidance, and strategies for managing fear and anxiety and can help individuals develop coping mechanisms and resilience.

Embrace Failure as a Learning Opportunity

Finally, it is important to embrace failure as a learning opportunity. Failing is a natural part of growth and learning, and it is important to view setbacks as opportunities for growth and improvement, rather than as reasons to give up.

In conclusion, overcoming fear and anxiety requires

identifying the root causes, challenging negative thoughts and beliefs, practicing mindfulness and self-care, seeking professional help, and embracing failure as a learning opportunity. By implementing these strategies, individuals can reduce fear and anxiety, increase resilience, and achieve their goals.

ᐁᐁᐁ

"Believe you can and you're halfway there."

- Theodore Roosevelt

ᗡᗡᗡ

SIX

ESTABLISHING A POSITIVE MINDSET

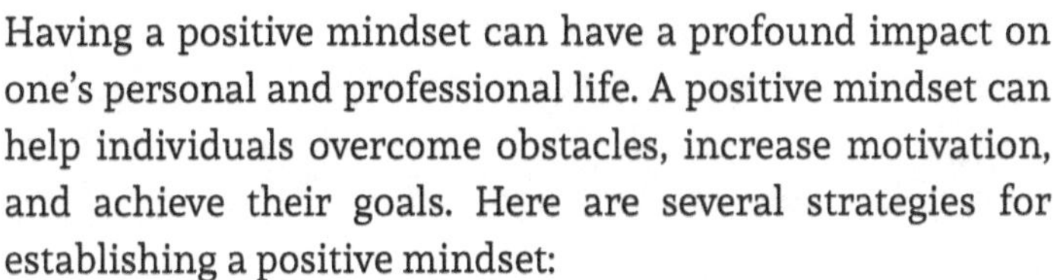

Having a positive mindset can have a profound impact on one's personal and professional life. A positive mindset can help individuals overcome obstacles, increase motivation, and achieve their goals. Here are several strategies for establishing a positive mindset:

Practice Gratitude

Practicing gratitude by focusing on what one has, rather than what one lacks, can help to shift perspective and increase positivity. This can involve keeping a gratitude journal, expressing gratitude to others, or simply taking time to reflect on the positive aspects of one's life.

Cultivate a Growth Mindset

Having a growth mindset, or the belief that one's abilities and intelligence can be developed through hard work and dedication, can increase resilience and motivation. This mindset can help individuals view challenges and failures as opportunities for growth, rather than as reasons to give up.

Surround Yourself with Positive Influences

Surrounding oneself with positive, supportive individuals can have a powerful impact on one's mindset. These individuals can offer encouragement, support, and positive perspective, and can help to counteract negative influences.

Engage in Positive Self-Talk

Positive self-talk, or speaking kindly and positively to oneself, can have a profound impact on one's mindset and overall well-being. This can involve reframing negative thoughts, focusing on one's strengths, and speaking kindly to oneself, even in challenging situations.

Embrace Positive Habits

Finally, embracing positive habits, such as exercise, meditation, or reading, can help to establish a positive mindset and improve overall well-being. By incorporating these habits into one's routine, individuals can cultivate a more positive outlook and increase motivation and productivity.

In conclusion, establishing a positive mindset involves practicing gratitude, cultivating a growth mindset, surrounding oneself with positive influences, engaging in positive self-talk, and embracing positive habits. By implementing these strategies, individuals can increase positivity, resilience, and motivation, and achieve their goals.

ԾԾԾ

"*I am not a product of my circumstances. I am a product of my decisions.*"

- **Stephen Covey**

❥❥❥

SEVEN

DEVELOPING SELF-DISCIPLINE

Self-discipline is a key component of self-motivation and is essential for achieving goals. It involves the ability to control one's impulses and make decisions that align with one's goals and values, even in the face of temptation or distraction. Here are several strategies for developing self-discipline:

Identify Priorities

The first step in developing self-discipline is to identify one's priorities. This involves clarifying what is most important and what one is willing to sacrifice in order to achieve their goals.

Create a Routine

Creating a routine can help to establish structure and consistency, and can provide a sense of stability and direction. This can involve setting a schedule, planning out tasks and responsibilities, and dedicating specific times to specific activities.

Set Realistic Goals

Setting realistic goals, and breaking down larger goals into smaller, more manageable steps, can help to increase motivation and reduce the risk of feeling overwhelmed.

Eliminate Distractions

Eliminating distractions, such as turning off notifications, setting boundaries, and creating a designated workspace, can help to increase focus and productivity.

Practice Delayed Gratification

Delayed gratification involves the ability to resist temptation and delay pleasure or reward in order to achieve a larger goal. This can involve setting aside short-term desires in order to pursue long-term goals, and can help to build self-discipline and increase motivation.

Hold Yourself Accountable

Finally, holding oneself accountable is essential to developing self-discipline. This may involve setting up an accountability system, such as tracking progress or seeking support from others, or making a commitment to stick to one's goals and priorities.

In conclusion, developing self-discipline involves identifying priorities, creating a routine, setting realistic goals, eliminating distractions, practicing delayed gratification, and holding oneself accountable. By incorporating these strategies, individuals can increase self-discipline, motivation, and the ability to achieve their goals.

ppp

"Successful people do what unsuccessful
people are not willing to do."

- Eric Thomas

❥❥❥

EIGHT

Understanding the Power of Habits

Habits play a powerful role in shaping our lives and can have a significant impact on our self-motivation and ability to achieve our goals. Here are several key points to consider when understanding the power of habits:

Habits are Automatic

Habits are actions that are performed automatically, without conscious thought. This makes them powerful, as they can be both helpful and harmful, depending on their nature.

Habits are Formed through Repetition

Habits are formed through repetition, and the more often a behavior is performed, the stronger the habit becomes. This means that habits can be difficult to change, but that they can also be harnessed to support self-motivation and goal achievement.

Habits Can Be Both Helpful and Harmful

Habits can be both helpful and harmful, depending on their nature. For example, a habit of exercise can be beneficial for one's health and motivation, while a habit of procrastination can hinder progress and success.

Habits Can Be Changed

Habits can be changed, but it requires intentional effort and persistence. This may involve replacing a harmful habit with a beneficial one, or simply breaking down a habit into smaller, more manageable steps.

Habits Impact Self-Motivation

Habits can have a significant impact on self-motivation, as they can either support or hinder progress and success. For example, a habit of consistent and intentional effort can increase motivation and help to achieve goals, while a habit of procrastination can undermine self-motivation and reduce progress.

In conclusion, habits play a powerful role in shaping our lives and can have a significant impact on our self-motivation and ability to achieve our goals. By understanding the nature of habits, and by intentionally forming and maintaining habits that support self-motivation and goal achievement, individuals can harness the power of habits to achieve their full potential.

❧❧❧

"The greatest glory in living lies not in never falling, but in rising every time we fall."

- Nelson Mandela

ᗡᗡᗡ

NINE

THE ROLE OF POSITIVE SELF-TALK

Positive self-talk refers to the practice of speaking to oneself in a positive and supportive manner, and it can play a crucial role in shaping self-motivation and success. Here are several key points to consider when understanding the role of positive self-talk:

Positive Self-Talk Impacts Emotions and Attitudes

Positive self-talk can have a significant impact on emotions and attitudes, as it helps to counteract negative thoughts and beliefs, and promotes a more positive outlook. This can help to increase self-motivation and confidence, and support the pursuit of goals.

Positive Self-Talk Shapes Self-Image

Positive self-talk can shape the way we see ourselves, and can help to build self-esteem and confidence. This can help to increase motivation, and make it easier to pursue and achieve goals.

Positive Self-Talk Supports Goal Achievement

Positive self-talk can help to support goal achievement, as it can increase motivation and reduce the impact of obstacles and setbacks. This can help individuals to stay focused on their goals, and to persist in the face of challenges.

Positive Self-Talk Helps Overcome Negative Thoughts and Beliefs

Positive self-talk can help to overcome negative thoughts and beliefs, and promote a more positive outlook. This can help individuals to increase their self-motivation and to stay focused on their goals, even in the face of adversity.

Positive Self-Talk is a Learned Skill

Positive self-talk is a learned skill, and can be developed through intentional practice and repetition. This may involve monitoring one's thoughts and replacing negative self-talk with positive affirmations, or engaging in positive visualization exercises.

In conclusion, positive self-talk plays a crucial role in shaping self-motivation and success, and can help individuals to overcome negative thoughts and beliefs, increase self-esteem and confidence, and support the pursuit and achievement of goals. By intentionally engaging in positive self-talk, individuals can harness its power to achieve their full potential.

❦❦❦

"The only way to do great work is to love what you do."

- Steve Jobs

♥♥♥

TEN

FINDING AND USING YOUR INNER STRENGTH

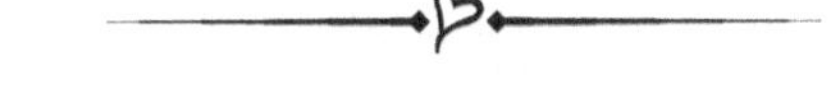

Inner strength refers to the qualities and abilities within an individual that support resilience and determination in the face of challenges and obstacles. Here are several key points to consider when finding and using your inner strength:

Identifying Your Inner Strengths

The first step in using your inner strength is to identify your strengths and areas of personal power. This may involve exploring personal interests, values, and skills, as well as considering past experiences and accomplishments.

Building Self-Awareness

Self-awareness is an important aspect of inner strength, and involves understanding your own thoughts, feelings, and behaviors. By building self-awareness, individuals can gain greater insight into their inner strengths, and can better understand how to harness them to achieve their goals.

Cultivating Mindfulness

Mindfulness is the practice of being present and fully engaged in the moment, and it can play a key role in supporting inner strength. By cultivating mindfulness, individuals can increase their self-awareness, and can better understand their own strengths and limitations.

Embracing Your Emotions

Embracing your emotions, both positive and negative, can help to increase inner strength and resilience. By acknowledging and accepting emotions, individuals can better understand their own experiences, and can develop a greater sense of self-awareness and inner strength.

Building Positive Relationships

Positive relationships with others can provide support and encouragement, and can help to increase inner strength. By building positive relationships, individuals can tap into the strength and support of others, and can better understand their own strengths and weaknesses.

Engaging in Self-Care

Self-care is an important aspect of inner strength, and involves taking care of one's physical, emotional, and psychological well-being. This may involve engaging in activities such as exercise, mindfulness, or spending time with loved ones.

In conclusion, finding and using your inner strength involves developing self-awareness, embracing your emotions, building positive relationships, and engaging in self-care. By harnessing the power of inner strength, individuals can increase their resilience and determination, and can achieve their goals with greater ease and success.

ᐁᐁᐁ

"Self-motivation is the key to success."

- Tony Robbins

❥❥❥

ELEVEN

Reaching Your Goals Through Visualization

Visualization is the practice of using imagination and mental imagery to create a clear and vivid picture of a desired outcome or goal. Here are several key points to consider when using visualization to reach your goals:

Clarity and Specificity

To effectively use visualization, it is important to have a clear and specific picture of the desired outcome or goal. This may involve setting specific, measurable, and achievable goals, and creating a vivid and detailed image of what success looks like.

Emotion and Feeling

Visualization is most effective when it is accompanied by

strong emotions and feelings. By attaching positive emotions and feelings to the mental image of the desired outcome or goal, individuals can increase their motivation and commitment to achieving it.

Consistency and Frequency

Visualization is most effective when it is practiced consistently and frequently. This may involve setting aside time each day to practice visualization, and incorporating it into daily routines and habits.

Affirmations and Self-Talk

Affirmations and positive self-talk can be powerful tools for enhancing the effectiveness of visualization. By using affirmations and positive self-talk to reinforce the mental image of the desired outcome or goal, individuals can increase their confidence and motivation.

Action and Implementation

Visualization is most effective when it is accompanied by action and implementation. This may involve taking specific and meaningful steps towards achieving the desired outcome or goal, and following through with the plan.

Celebrating Successes

Celebrating successes, no matter how small, can help to reinforce the power of visualization and increase motivation and commitment. By acknowledging and celebrating successes along the way, individuals can maintain momentum and stay focused on their goals.

In conclusion, reaching your goals through visualization involves having a clear and specific picture of the desired outcome, attaching positive emotions and feelings to the mental image, practicing visualization consistently and frequently, using affirmations and positive self-talk, taking action and implementing a plan, and celebrating successes along the way. By harnessing the power of visualization, individuals can increase their motivation, focus, and commitment to achieving their goals.

"Success is not a destination, it's a journey."

- Zig Ziglar

❥❥❥

TWELVE

MAKING A COMMITMENT TO YOURSELF

Making a commitment to yourself is an important step towards achieving your goals and realizing your full potential. Here are several key points to consider when making a commitment to yourself:

Define Your Goals and Values

It is important to start by defining your goals and values. This may involve writing down a list of goals, prioritizing them, and determining what values and beliefs are most important to you.

Create a Plan

Once you have defined your goals and values, the next step is to create a plan for achieving them. This may involve setting specific, measurable, and achievable goals, and developing a roadmap for reaching those goals.

Be Accountable

Making a commitment to yourself requires accountability. This may involve enlisting the support of a friend, family member, or accountability partner, and regularly reviewing your progress and making adjustments as needed.

Practice Self-Care

Self-care is an important component of making a commitment to yourself. This may involve setting aside time each day for activities that support physical, emotional, and mental well-being, such as exercise, mindfulness, and relaxation.

Stay Focused and Committed

Staying focused and committed to your goals requires a strong commitment to personal growth and development. This may involve setting aside time each day for reflection and introspection, and seeking out opportunities for learning and growth.

Celebrate Your Successes

Celebrating your successes, no matter how small, is an important component of making a commitment to yourself. By acknowledging and celebrating your achievements, you can reinforce your commitment and stay motivated.

In conclusion, making a commitment to yourself involves defining your goals and values, creating a plan, being accountable, practicing self-care, staying focused and committed, and celebrating your successes. By making a commitment to yourself, you can increase your motivation, focus, and commitment to achieving your goals and realizing your full potential.

ppp

"You miss 100% of the shots you don't take."

- Wayne Gretzky

▷▷▷

THIRTEEN

THE ROLE OF SELF-CARE AND SELF-LOVE

Self-care and self-love are important components of self-motivation and play a critical role in helping you reach your goals and live a fulfilling life. Here are several key points to consider when it comes to self-care and self-love:

The Importance of Self-Care

Self-care refers to taking care of your physical, emotional, and mental well-being. This may involve engaging in activities that support your overall health and well-being, such as exercise, healthy eating, and getting enough rest and sleep.

The Connection between Self-Care and Self-Love

Self-care and self-love are closely connected. When you

engage in self-care activities, you are showing love and respect for yourself, which can lead to greater self-confidence and self-esteem.

The Benefits of Self-Love

Self-love can bring many benefits, including increased happiness, better relationships, and improved physical health. When you love and accept yourself, you are more likely to set and achieve your goals, and to feel more confident and motivated.

Engaging in Self-Care Activities

There are many ways to engage in self-care and self-love, such as setting aside time for yourself each day, practicing mindfulness, journaling, and seeking out support and connection with others.

Overcoming Obstacles to Self-Care

Obstacles to self-care and self-love may include feelings of guilt, shame, or low self-esteem. To overcome these obstacles, it is important to practice self-compassion, and to seek out support and guidance from a trusted friend, family member, or therapist.

The Role of Gratitude and Positive Self-Talk

Gratitude and positive self-talk can also play a role in self-care and self-love. By focusing on what you are thankful for and speaking kindly to yourself, you can increase your motivation, focus, and commitment to self-care and self-love.

In conclusion, self-care and self-love are critical components of self-motivation, and play a crucial role in helping you reach your goals and live a fulfilling life. By engaging in self-care activities, overcoming obstacles, and focusing on gratitude and positive self-talk, you can increase your self-love, self-confidence, and motivation, and achieve your full potential.

ᐁᐁᐁ

"Successful people are not gifted, they just work hard and succeed on purpose."

- G.K. Nielson

❥❥❥

FOURTEEN

MEDITATION AS A TOOL FOR SELF-MOTIVATION

Meditation is a powerful tool that can help you increase your self-motivation and achieve your goals. Here are several key points to consider when it comes to meditation as a tool for self-motivation:

Understanding Meditation

Meditation is a practice that involves focusing your attention and calming your mind, usually by focusing on your breath or a specific object or sound. Regular meditation can help reduce stress, increase self-awareness, and boost focus and concentration.

The Benefits of Meditation for Self-Motivation

Meditation can be a valuable tool for self-motivation, as

it can help increase self-awareness, reduce stress, and improve focus and concentration. Additionally, meditation can help you develop a positive mindset, increase self-confidence, and overcome fears and anxiety.

Incorporating Meditation into Your Life

To incorporate meditation into your life, consider setting aside time each day for meditation practice, using guided meditations or apps to help you get started, and exploring different types of meditation, such as mindfulness or mantra meditation.

Overcoming Obstacles to Meditation

Obstacles to meditation may include feelings of boredom, frustration, or difficulty sitting still. To overcome these obstacles, it is important to be patient with yourself and to seek out support and guidance from a trusted friend, family member, or therapist.

The Role of Gratitude and Positive Self-Talk

Gratitude and positive self-talk can also play a role in meditation, as focusing on what you are thankful for and speaking kindly to yourself can increase your motivation, focus, and commitment to meditation practice.

In conclusion, meditation can be a powerful tool for self-motivation, as it can help increase self-awareness, reduce stress, improve focus and concentration, and develop a positive mindset. By incorporating meditation into your life, overcoming obstacles, and focusing on gratitude and positive self-talk, you can increase your self-motivation, self-confidence, and achieve your full potential.

ϷϷϷ

"The secret of success is to do the common things uncommonly well."

- John D. Rockefeller Jr.

▷▷▷

FIFTEEN

Evaluating and Adjusting Your Progress

Evaluating and adjusting your progress is an important part of achieving your goals and maintaining self-motivation. Here are several key points to consider when it comes to evaluating and adjusting your progress:

Measuring Progress

Measuring progress can help you assess your progress towards your goals and identify areas that may need improvement. This can be done through setting benchmarks, tracking your progress, and using tools like calendars, journals, or goal-setting apps.

The Importance of Regular Evaluation

Regular evaluation is essential for maintaining self-motivation and staying on track towards your goals. By regularly evaluating your progress, you can identify areas that need improvement, adjust your strategies, and celebrate your successes.

Adjusting Your Goals

Adjusting your goals is an important part of the progress-evaluation process, as it allows you to make changes to your strategies and approaches as needed. This may involve re-evaluating your goals, modifying your methods, and setting new benchmarks to help you stay on track.

Overcoming Setbacks

Setbacks are a normal part of the progress-evaluation process, and it is important to be prepared for them and have a plan for overcoming them. This may involve seeking support and guidance from trusted friends, family members, or therapists, and using positive self-talk and visualization to help you stay motivated and focused.

Celebrating Successes

Celebrating successes is an important part of the progress-evaluation process, as it helps to maintain self-motivation and reinforces positive behaviors. This may involve setting aside time to reflect on your achievements, recognizing your hard work and dedication, and treating yourself to a special activity or reward.

In conclusion, evaluating and adjusting your progress is a crucial part of achieving your goals and maintaining self-motivation. By regularly measuring your progress, adjusting your goals, overcoming setbacks, and celebrating successes, you can stay on track towards your goals and reach your full potential.

ᭇᭇᭇ

"*Success is not the key to happiness.
Happiness is the key to success.*"

- Albert Schweitzer

♥♥♥

Other Books Of The Author

1. The Moments When I Met God
2. Kashiyile Theertha Pathangal
3. GURU GYAN VANI
4. Abhiprerak Gita
5. ASSI SE JAIN GHAT TAK
6. Hopelessness of Arjuna
7. The Soul and It's True Nature
8. Sense of Action (Karma)
9. Action through Wisdom
10. Action through Wisdom
11. THEORY AND PRACTICAL OF EVERY ACTION
12. LOGICAL UNDERSTANDING OF THE SUPREME
13. THE IMPERISHABLE SUPREME
14. Yatra Nishadraj se Hanuman Ghat Tak
15. Yatra Karnatak Ghat se Raja Ghat Tak
16. Yatra Pandey Ghat se Prayagraj Ghat Tak
17. Yatra Ranjendra Prasad Ghat se Dattatreya Ghat Tak
18. YaatraSindhiya Ghat se Gwaliar Ghat Tak
19. Yatra Mangala Gauri Ghat se Hanuman Gadhi Ghat Tak
20. Yatra Gaay Ghat Se Nishad Ghat Tak
21. MAA GANGA, GHATEN EVM UTSAV
22. Ganga Arti Dev Deepavali evam Any Utsav
23. Potentials of Digitalized India
24. VEDIC CONSCIOUSNESS
25. A Brief Introduction to Vedic Science
26. Kashi ke Barah Jyotirling
27. IMPACT OF MOTIVATION
28. Let's have a Milky Way Journey
29. Color Therapy in a Nutshell

59. The Holistic Cow: A Look at the Physical, Spiritual, and Cultural Importance of Cows in India
60. Arts of Healing
61. Exploring the Divine
62. Understanding Five Elements
63. The Etymology of Ram
64. Symbols of India
65. Voice of Change (About Speeches of Great Men)
66. She Speaks (About Speeches of Great Women)
67. Patriotism on Celluloid – Brief About Patriotic Films
68. The Music of Motivation: A Brief Guide to Inspirational Film Songs
69. **Unlocking the Secrets of the Dashopanishads**
70. A Cultural Mosaic
71. Ancient Traditions, Modern Minds
72. Ecos of Ancient Wisdom
73. Beneath the Surface
74. From Temples to Ashrams
75. Sages of the Subcontinent
76. The Art of Healling (Ayurveda, Yoga & Naturopathy)
77. Indian Kitchen
78. The Festivals of India
79. The Indian Epics Retold
80. The Power of Mantras
81. The Indian River Ganges
82. The Indian Architecture
83. Rites of Passage
84. The Indian Silk Road
85. The Indian Literature
86. The Indian Villages
87. The Indian Folks & Crafts
88. The Way of Buddha
89. The Ramayan of Tulsidas

121. Innovative Startups - 25 Startup Ideas to Spark Your Business Creativity
122. Export Management: Strategies for Global Success
123. Exporting from India - A Step by Step Guide
124. Finance Fundamentals: Mastering Financial Management for Business Success
125. Global Growth Strategies for International Business Development
126. Marketing Mastery: Unlocking the Secrets of Modern Marketing
127. Operations Mastery: Managing the Flow of Value in Business
128. Strategic Business Management: Navigating the Modern Business Landscape
129. Human Resource Management Strategies for Building and Managing a High Performance Team
130. The Indian Landscapes and Nature: An Exploration Of India's Natural Beauty And Diversity
131. The Indian Street Performances: A Cultural Exploration of India's Street Performances
132. Affirming Your Self-Worth: Strategies for Achieving Emotional Wellbeing
133. Cultivating Self-Discipline: Secrets Methods for Achieving Your Goals
134. Embracing Change: Strategies for Adapting to Life's Challenges
135. Embracing Your Uniqueness: Secret Strategies for Living an Authentic Life
136. Finding Motivation in Despondency: Coping with Difficult Times

ppp

Contact

DR. JAGADEESH PILLAI

MBA & PhD in Vedic Science

Four Times Guinness World Record Holder

Winner of Mahatma Gandhi Vishwa Shanti Puraskar and
Global Peace Ambassador

Gemology, Astro & Vastu Consultant - Spiritual Counselor

Consultant for designing World Record Ideas

Efficient Tarot Card Reader

9839093003

myrichindia@gmail.com

drjagadeeshpillai@facebook

drjagadeeshpillai@instagram
jagadeeshpillai@youtube

www. JAGADEESHPILLAI.com

ᐩᐩᐩ

|| LOKAHA SAMASTHAHA SUKHINO BHAVANTU ||

❧❧❧

www.ingramcontent.com/pod-product-compliance
Lightning Source LLC
Chambersburg PA
CBHW031959140726
47988CB00019B/2739